D0456027

504

A TASTE OF CHICKEN SOUP

FOR THE

GOLFER'S SOUL

The 2nd Round

More Stories of Insight, Inspiration and Laughter on the Links

Jack Canfield, Mark Victor Hansen,
Jeffy Aubery, Mark & Chrissy Donnelly

Health Communications, Inc.
Deerfield Beach, Florida

www.hcibooks.com
www.chickensoup.com

The Man with the Perfect Swing. Reprinted by permission of Bruce Selcraig. ©2000 Bruce Selcraig.

Ladies, Is Golf for You? Reprinted by permission of Deisy M. Flood. ©1998 Deisy M. Flood. Appeared in *Golf Journal*, November/December 1998.

Golf's Ace with Heart. Reprinted by permission of Jolee Ann Edmondson. ©1982 Jolee Ann Edmondson.

The Spirit of Harvey Penick. Reprinted by permission of Leonard Finkel. ©2000 Leonard Finkel.

Snakes Alive! Reprinted by permission of *Golf Journal.* From *Golf Journal* issue October, 1991.

Fear of the Father-Son Tournament. Reprinted by permission of *Golf Journal.* From *Golf Journal* issue June, 2000.

The Y2K Crisis. Reprinted by permission of George Peper. ©1999 George Peper. Appeared in *Golf Magazine*, March 1999.

Thursday Is Men's Day. Reprinted with permission of Dan Jenkins. ©2000 Dan Jenkins. Appeared in *Golf Digest*, July 2000.

Humor at Its Best. Reprinted by permission of John Spielbergs. ©2001 John Spielbergs.

The Life and Times of a Golf Ball. Reprinted by permission of Robert P. Robinson. ©1971 Robert P. Robinson. Originally appeared in *Golf Journal* (USGA), May, 1971.

Library of Congress Cataloging-in-Publication Data is on file with the Library of Congress

© 2005 Jack Canfield and Mark Victor Hansen
ISBN 0-7573-0344-7

All rights reserved. Printed in the United States of America. No part of this publication may be reproduced, stored in a retrieval system or transmitted in any form or by any means, electronic, mechanical, photocopying, recording or otherwise, without the written permission of the publisher.

HCI, its Logos and Marks are trademarks of Health Communications, Inc.

Publisher: Health Communications Inc.
3201 SW 15th Street, Deerfield Beach, FL 33442

With honor and respect,
we dedicate this book
to the memory of
Payne Stewart,
and to the wonderful family
for whom he cared so much.

Contents

Introduction

Perhaps no moment in golf's long and illustrious history better exemplifies what it is about golf that captivates a player than the final match of the 1969 Ryder Cup. The most competitive matches in the history of the event, it all came down to the 18th hole on the final day, with Jack Nicklaus and Tony Jacklin both needing to sink their next putt for par. After Nicklaus, who was playing in his first Ryder Cup matches, holed out his four-footer, he graciously, and courageously, conceded Jacklin's two-footer to halve the round and result in the first tie in Ryder Cup history. That simple gesture embodied all that is good about golf, its reflective character and its glorious possibilities.

Jack Nicklaus, acting on behalf of all of us, looked in that mirror, and in that moment, on that illustrious day, the best of the human spirit smiled back. And in our humble estimation, that is *what it is about golf.*

The Man with the Perfect Swing

You must work very hard to become a natural golfer.

GARY PLAYER

On a warm morning at a country club near Orlando, a stocky gentleman with wispy gray hair makes his way past the crowd gathered for today's exhibition. To those who don't know better, the impish old fellow could be just another sunburned senior dreaming of bogey golf.

He wears a black turtleneck despite the heat. The left pocket of his neon-lime slacks bulges, as always, with two golf balls—never more, never fewer. All three watches on his left wrist are set to the same time.

Taking his position at the tee, he quickly lofts a few short wedge shots about 70 yards. At first the spectators seem unimpressed. Then they notice that the balls are landing on top of one another. "Every shot same as the last," chirps the golfer, as if to himself. "Same as the last."

Moving to a longer club, a 7-iron, he smoothly launches two dozen balls, which soar 150 yards and come to rest so close to each other you could cover them with a bedspread. He then pulls out his driver and sends a hail of balls 250 yards away—all clustered on a patch of grass the size of a two-car garage.

Astonished laughter erupts from the crowd. "Perfectly straight," says the golfer in a singsong voice. "There it goes. Perfectly straight."

People who have followed Moe Norman's career are no longer surprised by his uncanny displays of accuracy. Many professionals and avid players consider the seventy-year-old Canadian a near-mythical figure. But few outside the sport have ever heard his name. Fewer still know the story of his struggle to find acceptance in the only world he understands.

One cold January morning in 1935, five-year-old Murray Norman was sledding double with a friend on an ice-packed hillside near his home in Kitchener, Ontario. Speeding downhill, the sled hurtled into the street and skidded under a passing car.

Both boys survived and ran home crying. But the car's right rear tire had rolled over Moe's head, pushing up the cheekbone on one side of his face. His parents, unable to afford medical care, could only pray he did not suffer serious brain injury.

As Moe grew older, he developed odd behavioral quirks and a repetitive, staccato speech pattern. His older brother Ron noticed that Moe seemed unusually frightened of unfamiliar situations. At night, Ron often heard his little brother sobbing in bed, devastated by some real or imagined slight.

At school Moe felt glaringly out of place among other kids. Desperate for friends and acceptance, he tried to be playful, but his efforts often backfired—pinching people too hard or bear hugging them until they pushed him away. He heaped ridicule on himself and even coined his own nickname: Moe the Schmoe.

He became known as a slow student in every subject—except one. At math no one could touch Moe Norman. He astounded his classmates by memorizing complicated problems and multiplying two-digit numbers in his head almost instantly.

When he wasn't acting the clown, Moe walled himself off from others. Over time he plunged deeper into isolation, and yet, ironically, loneliness led him to his greatest happiness.

In the years following his accident, Moe spent hours atop that same winter sledding hill, hacking around an old golf ball with a rusty, wood-shafted 5-iron he found at home. Here in the solitary and magical world of golf, he found a reason to wake up each morning.

Kitchener, Ontario, in the 1940s was a gritty factory town where working-class teenagers had little desire or money to play the "sissy," upper-class game of golf. But Moe was spellbound, often skipping meals, school and chores to head off by himself in a field to hit balls—five hundred or more a day. He practiced until dark, sometimes until the blood from his hands made the club too slippery to hold.

In his early teens Moe landed a job as a caddie at a country club—only to be fired when he hurled the clubs of a low-tipping local mogul into some trees. Soon he gave up caddying to concentrate on playing, honing his skills at a nearby public golf course. He quit school in tenth grade, and by the time he was nineteen, he knew he was blessed with a rare talent: He could hit a golf ball wherever he wanted it to go.

Moe left home in his early twenties, hitching rides to compete in amateur golf tournaments all over Canada, supporting himself with a succession of low-paying jobs. At his first few tournaments in the late 1940s, fans didn't know what to make of the odd little fellow with the garish, mismatched outfits, strawlike red hair and crooked teeth.

His manner was playful, almost childlike, his self-taught technique wildly unorthodox. Legs spread wide, he stood over the ball like a slugger at the plate, clutching the club not with his fingers, as most golfers are taught to do, but tightly in his palms, wrists cocked, as if he were holding a sledgehammer.

Many spectators dismissed him as an amusing sideshow. Some giggled when he stepped up to the tee. Soon, though, Moe Norman was turning heads for reasons other than his personal style.

Recognized as a gifted player who could hit a golf ball with breathtaking precision, he quickly became a sensation on the amateur golf circuit. In one year alone he shot 61 four times, set nine course records and won seventeen out of twenty-six tournaments.

Even as his fame grew, Moe remained painfully shy and could not shake the sense that he was undeserving of the attention. Rather than bask in the spotlight, he avoided it. In 1955, after winning the Canadian Amateur Open in Calgary, Moe failed to show for the awards ceremony. Friends later found him by the nearby Elbow River, cooling his feet.

That victory qualified Moe for one of golf's most prestigious events: the Masters. When the invitation to the tournament arrived, he was only twenty-six and spending his winters setting pins in a Kitchener bowling alley. The Masters was his chance not only to represent his country but to show skeptics he wasn't just some freak on a run of beginner's luck.

But his old demons would give him no rest. Moe felt like an intruder among some of golf's bright lights. He played miserably in the first round and even worse on day two. So he fled to a nearby driving range to practice.

While hitting balls Moe noticed someone behind him. "Mind if I give you a little tip?" asked Sam Snead. The Hall-of-Famer merely suggested a slight change in his long-iron stroke.

But for Moe it was like Moses bringing the Eleventh Commandment down from the mountaintop.

Determined to put Snead's advice to good use, Moe stayed on the range until dark, hitting balls by the hundreds. His hands became raw and blistered. The next day, unable to hold a club, he withdrew from the Masters, humiliated.

But Moe climbed right back up the ladder to win the Canadian Amateur again a year later. A string of victories followed. In time, he had won so many tournaments and collected so many televisions, wristwatches and other prizes that he began selling off those he didn't want.

When the Royal Canadian Golf Association charged him with accepting donations for travel expenses, which was against regulations for amateurs, Moe decided to turn professional. His first move as a pro was to enter, and win, the Ontario Open.

As a newcomer to professional golf, Moe approached the game with the same impish lightheartedness of his amateur years. When people laughed, he played along by acting the clown. An extremely fast player, he'd set up and make his shot in about three seconds, then sometimes stretch out on the fairway and pretend to doze until the other players caught up.

Fans loved the show, but some of his fellow competitors on the U.S. PGA Tour did not. At the Los Angeles Open in 1959, a small group of players cornered Moe in the locker room. "Stop goofing off," they told him, demanding that he improve his technique as well as his wardrobe.

Friends say a shadow fell across Moe that

day. Some believe the episode shattered his self-confidence and persuaded him to back out of the American tour, never to return. More than anything, Moe had wanted to be accepted by the players he so admired. But he was unlike the others, and now he was being punished for it.

The laughter suddenly seemed barbed and personal. No longer could he shrug it off when some jerk in the galleries mimicked his high-pitched voice or hitched up his waistline to mock Moe's too-short trousers.

Because Moe never dueled the likes of Americans Jack Nicklaus or Arnold Palmer, he achieved little recognition beyond Canada. At home, though, his success was staggering. On the Canadian PGA Tour and in smaller events in Florida, Moe won fifty-four tournaments and set thirty-three course records. While most world-class golfers count their lifetime holes-in-one on a few fingers, Moe has scored at least seventeen.

Despite his fame and the passing years, Moe was continually buffeted by the mood swings that tormented him in childhood.

Even among friends he could be curt, sometimes embarrassingly rude.

At other times he was charming, lovable Moe, bear hugging friends and tossing golf balls to children like candy—the happy-go-lucky clown from his amateur days.

Through the 1960s and '70s, Moe racked up one tournament victory after another. But in the early 1980s his enthusiasm for competition began to wane. His winnings dwindled, and he slipped into depression. Not being wealthy, he seemed to care very little for money, lending thousands to aspiring golfers and never bothering to collect.

Broke and all but forgotten, he drifted from shabby apartments and boarding-houses to cut-rate roadside motels, often sleeping in his car. Had it not been for the generosity of friends—and a stroke of good luck—he might have faded entirely into obscurity.

Moe has never had a telephone, a credit card or owned a house. Few people know where he might be living on any given day, and he seldom talks to strangers. Little wonder it took Jack Kuykendall two years to track him down.

Kuykendall, founder of a company called Natural Golf Corp., finally caught up with him in Titusville, Florida. He told Moe that, trained in physics, he had worked for years to develop the perfect golf swing—only to discover that an old-timer from Canada had been using the same technique for forty years. He had to meet this man.

Moe agreed to demonstrate his swing at clinics sponsored by Natural Golf Corp. Word spread quickly through the golfing grapevine, and before long, sports magazines were trumpeting the mysterious genius with the killer swing.

Among those following Moe's story was Wally Uihlein, president of the golf-ball company Titleist and FootJoy Worldwide. Hoping to preserve one of golf's treasures, Uihlein announced in 1995 that his company was awarding Norman five thousand dollars a month for the rest of his life. Stunned, Moe asked what he had to do to earn the money. "Nothing," said Uihlein. "You've already done it."

Two weeks later, Moe Norman was elected to the Canadian Golf Hall of Fame. Even today, however, he remains largely unknown outside his native country except among true disciples of the game. For them, Moe is golf's greatest unsung hero, the enigmatic loner once described by golfer Lee Trevino as "the best ball-striker I ever saw come down the pike." Many agree with Jack Kuykendall—had someone given Moe a hand forty years ago, "we would know his name like we know Babe Ruth's."

In the parking lot of a Florida country club, Moe Norman is leaning into his gray Cadillac, fumbling through a pile of motivational tapes. He seems nervous and rushed, but as he slides behind the wheel, he pauses to reflect on his life, his family and his obsession.

Moe never had a real mentor or a trusted advisor. "Today's kids," he says, "are driven right up to the country club. Nice golf shoes, twenty-dollar gloves, nice pants. 'Have a nice day, Son.' I cry when I hear that. Oooh, if I'd ever heard that when I was growing up . . ."

He squints into the sun and cocks his head. "Everyone wanted me to be happy their way," he says. "But I did it my way. Now, every night I sit in the corner of my room in the dark before I go to bed and say, 'My life belongs to me. My life belongs to me.'"

With that, he shuts the door and rolls down the window just a crack. Asked where he's going, Moe brightens instantly, and a look of delight spreads across his face.

"Gone to hit balls," he says, pulling away. "Hit balls."

It is, and forever will be, the highlight of his day.

Bruce Selcraig

Ladies, Is Golf for You?

Our minds need relaxation, and give way
Unless we mix with work a little play.

MOLIÉRE

I took up the game of golf eight years ago when I was at the age of . . . never mind. I became so addicted to the game, I didn't have time to do the laundry anymore. Soon after, my husband had a plaque made for me that says "Martha Stewart Used to Live Here." Sometimes I'd have to stop on my way home after a round of golf to buy him a pair of underwear for work the next day. He has two drawers full of BVDs. God forbid, but if he's ever in an accident, not only will he be wearing clean underwear, most likely it'll be brand-new.

Golf is great, but I can still remember what a frustrating experience it can be for the beginner. For the first three months, I wondered if golf was my punishment for the time I sneaked into Sister Mary Margaret's bedroom to see if she really had a poster of Bob Dylan hanging over her bed. That was the rumor around school. I cried so much as a beginning golfer, my husband suggested I have my hormone level checked. He couldn't believe it was just golf doing it. But I persevered and things became better, and so now I would like to share some tips and ideas that can make a woman's initial foray into golf a little smoother.

Whatever your reasons for taking up the game, whether it's to avoid listening to your son practice the French horn or to get away from your mother-in-law, ask yourself a few questions to see if this game is really your bag. You may be athletic, but there's more than skill involved here.

Temperament, for instance. If you have a hair-trigger kind of temper, occasionally coupled with a bad case of anxiety, a club in your hands that particular day can be dangerous. I once saw a woman do quite a number on the 150-yard marker, a pretty shrub in bloom, with her 7-iron just because her favorite pink ball went into the lake.

Vanity. Particularly in the summer. If you worry about your hair flopping on humid days, your foundation running until your face looks like it's melting, or your mascara making black tracks down your cheeks, stay at home and make pot holders.

Prudery. If you're the kind of person easily offended by less-than-ladylike words, forget it.

But before you spend a fortune on clubs and figure out six months later that what you really want to do is skydive, I suggest you borrow most, if not all, the essentials first. You'll need clubs (up to fourteen, eight of which look exactly alike, but in a few years you'll be able to tell the difference), a bag, shoes (the ones with plastic spikes for traction), balls, tees, a towel and a ball marker (a quarter will do, but don't forget to pick it up when you leave the green).

If your friends don't have a spare set of clubs to loan out, you can find used clubs at garage sales or pawn shops at reasonable prices. Buy something cheap for now. At this point, equipment doesn't matter much since you have no idea what you're doing.

Eventually, if you stick with the game, you'll find yourself buying a new driver all the time. Every time you hear about another that can help you hit the ball ten more yards, you'll go and buy it. I've noticed that no matter who the manufacturer is or what the club material, it's always "an extra ten yards." You'd think, out of all the clubmakers, one company would have an engineer smart enough to come up with a club that'll give us fifty extra yards and get it over with for a while.

I love drivers. They're all so different. They come in persimmon, graphite, titanium, with bubbles, without bubbles, large heads, extra-large heads, stiff and extra-stiff shafts—you name it.

Now once you have your equipment, you need an instructor. But ladies: Do not let your husband teach you. When was the last time you listened to him anyway? What makes you think you're going to start now? Sooner or later even his voice will start grating on your nerves. Trust me, it won't work. Find yourself a real pro. My guess is that the person who said sex is one of the main sources of disagreements between couples didn't teach his wife the game of golf.

One more piece of advice: While you're still a beginner, don't play in events for couples if the format is that of alternate shot. Heaven help if your shot lands directly behind a tree, on top of a root or in a bunker in a "fried egg" lie and now he has to play it. That's an argument waiting to happen. And it will happen.

Another thought to keep in mind for the sake of keeping peace at home: If you ever hit a hole-in-one, never mention it again after the day it happens. I've had two, and he hasn't even one. I love my husband too much to upset him, so I don't talk about them in his presence. But my plaques hang in the den, one on each side of the television, where he can see them every night. I also have a vanity license plate, 2-HOLS-N-1— and he washes my car every Saturday.

Golf's like fishing: There's always the one that got away. In golf there's always the putt that didn't fall. But there's more to golf than making good shots. Fun moments that don't have anything to do with the game can happen on the course. There was the time when my husband uncharacteristically threw his sand wedge after shanking a short chip. The grip hit the cart path first, propelling the club into a 360-degree rotation and directly into the golf bag. Eventually, you'll have your own stories to tell, and you'll remember them years from now.

Above all else, have fun, even on those days when you feel you should have stayed home making those pot holders instead of going to the course, accomplishing nothing more than achieving that dreaded tan line that makes your feet look like you're wearing bobby socks with high heels in your finest evening gown.

Golf can be played long after you start collecting your first Social Security check. When you reach that age, you can start making cute ball markers and tee holders to give your friends at Christmas. By the way, did you know the Senior Tour has players in their seventies? Ladies don't have a Senior Tour. They won't admit when they turn fifty. It's a woman thing.

Deisy Flood

Golf's Ace with Heart

I try to use a method I call the positive-negative approach. I positively identify the negatives and work from there.

BOB MURPHY

It was another tournament town, another cardboard hotel room, another evening spent staring at the too-blue, too-orange television images atop the Formica-covered bureau. Juan "Chi Chi" Rodriquez, vying for the lead at the 1967 Texas Open in San Antonio, was practicing putts on the carpet and thinking about the birdies that slipped away that afternoon.

The drone of the evening news suddenly riveted his attention: a reporter was interviewing a distraught woman whose home in Illinois had been destroyed by a tornado. All she had left were the clothes she wore. Rodriguez was so moved that he made a pact with himself. If he bagged the trophy the following day, he would send the tornado relief fund five thousand dollars. The next day he won—and so did the tornado victims.

Across the country, dozens of people have benefited from the compassion of this pencil-thin Puerto Rican golf pro. While some professional athletes spend their spare time doing beer commercials, Rodriguez checks up on things like incurable diseases, child abuse and world hunger.

Everybody on tour knows about his big heart, even the caddies. After each of his eight tournament wins, he has staged a lavish dinner party for them. "Chi Chi makes us feel we really count," says veteran tour caddie Richard Holzer.

Rodriguez's benevolence has perhaps detracted from his golf game. For a man who once outdrove Jack Nicklaus by one hundred yards and is regarded by Ken Venturi as one of golf's finest shotmakers, there should be more than eight titles, and his career earnings should have soared beyond $1 million. But Rodriguez's mind was on other things.

"He'll never be as great a golfer as he is a human being," asserts pro Bill Kratzert. "Sometimes he worries more about what's happening in Asia than what's happening on the course. During practice he talks incessantly about poverty overseas."

At age forty-six in 1979, Rodriguez continued to play the PGA Tour nonstop while other pros his age were retiring. Although he hadn't won an event in three years, he zealously pursued a comeback. The reason: He planned to give his next winner's check to Mother Teresa for her leper colony in India.

Rodriguez came from a background riddled with the kind of despair he empathizes with today. He knows the feeling of a stomach aching with emptiness. Remembering is one of the things Chi Chi does best.

Rio Piedras is a poverty-scarred village just outside San Juan, Puerto Rico. Chickens and naked toddlers and skeletal dogs mingle around shacks alongside dirt roads where Chi Chi Rodriguez grew up.

One of six children, Chi Chi labored in the

sugar-cane plantations with his father, from whom he learned sensitivity, goodness and hope. "My dad worked fourteen hours a day, every day of his life." Rodriguez recalls. "He would come home dead-tired and hungry, but if he saw a kid walk by with a big belly—the sign of malnutrition—he'd give him his rice and beans. He did that so often I was concerned he wasn't getting enough to eat, but he always told me that God would supply him with strength."

Little time was available for recreation, but occasionally Chi Chi and his older brother would push each other down the highway in a cart. One day they crested a hill, rolled to the bottom—and discovered golf: "We saw this very green grass and men hitting tiny white balls with shiny steel sticks. I figured the guys who carried the bags for the players made money. It looked easier than being a waterboy at the plantation."

Rodriguez was only seven, but he marched across the stately fairways of Berwind Country Club and asked about a job lugging "those bags." The caddiemaster told him he was too small and suggested he start as a forecaddie, the person who marks the position of a player's ball and searches for errant golf balls. Chi Chi eagerly accepted.

Along the way he invented his own version of golf. For a club he attached a pipe to a guava limb, and for a ball he shaped a tin can into a sphere; then he dug a few holes to "play." Soon he could drive fifty to one hundred yards. All those swipes with guava limbs developed tremendous hand action, eventually making the 135-pound Rodriguez one of golf's longest hitters.

Caddies were prohibited from playing Berwind, but sometimes, just before nightfall, Chi Chi would sneak onto the turf with borrowed clubs and play eighteen holes in forty-five minutes. On occasion, he was trailed by an irate greenskeeper, who took potshots at him with a revolver. "I'd hit and run," Rodriguez remembers. (He is still one of pro golf's fastest players.) When he was only twelve, Chi Chi scored an astonishing 67 and knew golf was his future.

At the entrance of Berwind was an old Banyan tree that provided a perch for Rodriguez between shifts. There he watched the Cadillacs drive by and dreamed of the day he would be rich and waving to throngs of fans.

Rodriguez enlisted in the army at nineteen, making a name for himself in military golf tournaments during his two-year stint. After his discharge, he worked for a year as an aide at a psychiatric hospital in San Juan. He fed and bathed patients, played dominoes with them, calmed them when they became violent. The job was menial, paying eighty dollars a month, but Chi Chi calls it "the most rewarding work I've ever had. I was *giving,* and there's nothing more enjoyable than that."

He hadn't forgotten his dream, however, and he found the key to it in 1957, when the Dorado Beach Resort opened. Among its amenities was Puerto Rico's first pro- caliber golf course. Chi Chi headed there with a bundle of clippings about his army golf triumphs. Ed Dudley, the pro at the new course, was bringing a man from the states to assist him, but he grudgingly agreed that he and Chi Chi could play a game.

Rodriguez was so nervous that he shot an 89. "Mr. Dudley, I played awful today," he said, "but if you help me, I could become one of the best golfers in the world." Dudley looked off in the distance, then said, "Okay, you've got a job." And for the next three years Chi Chi worked for Dudley and Pete Cooper. Both men nurtured his potential, coaching him several hours a day.

When he was twenty-five, Rodriguez joined the Tour. From the start he made a comfortable income, and soon he was taking home trophies. He was a pacesetter when it came to injecting the bland pro-golf caravan with humor. "Americans are so hard-working," he explains, "and half of them don't enjoy their work. So I try to give them something to smile about when they come out to watch us."

As a successful golf pro, Rodriguez bought the big, shiny car he'd dreamed about in the Banyan tree, and a sprawling villa at Dorado Beach, too. But before he indulged in these trappings, he sent his brother through law school and bought homes for his mother and other family members. "This is the first house house we've had," says Iwalani, Chi Chi's Hawaiian-born wife. "Until three years ago, we lived out of suitcases. When he'd give away money to strangers, I'd think, 'We don't even have a place to call our own yet!'" Says Chi Chi, "When someone hurts, I hurt. It's tough being poor, and it's so easy to say, 'Well, I made it, so can everybody.' That just isn't true. Thousands of people don't have a chance."

Young people are more and more the focus of the golfer's generosity. The Chi Chi Rodriguez Youth Foundation, a nonprofit organization based in Clearwater, Florida, draws most of his charitable energies. Established to help troubled or abused youngsters, the foundation provides a program designed as a springboard into the free-enterprise system that also includes intensive academic tutoring and lots of golf instruction. They go on field trips to see how various businesses are run and to museums and sports events.

"Basically, these kids have been defeated all their lives," says Chi Chi. "So we're introducing them to challenges and positive competition, showing them that they can succeed."

During the 1979 J.C. Penney Golf Classic in Tampa, Florida, Rodriguez became interested in the project. Some youngsters from a juvenile detention center approached him for autographs. "The next thing I knew," recalls Bill Hayes, the counselor accompanying them, "Chi Chi was offering to come out and do a golf clinic. He arrived a few days later and hit balls over the prison walls. Afterward, he sat in the cells talking with the kids and ate dinner with them." That's when Hayes outlined to Rodriguez the plans for the Youth Foundation. Today 450 youngsters are enrolled.

Meanwhile, back home, Chi Chi's kind touch is felt by the Children's Hospital of Puerto Rico, which his annual tournament—the Chi Chi Rodriguez International Festival of Golf—continues to benefit.

But it's not just the sweeping gestures Chi Chi is known for. "If someone is hurting," points out Bill Braddock, a longtime friend, "Chi Chi's going to try to help. It wouldn't surprise me at all if he gave up golf and started making house calls."

Jolee Edmondson

[EDITORS' NOTE: *Ranked fourth on the Senior Tour's all-time victory list, Chi Chi continues to devote his energies to his youth foundation, which currently serves over five hundred kids.*]

The Spirit of Harvey Penick

My father says to me, "Respect everybody, and your life, it will be perfect." Then, even if you are poor on the outside, on the inside you are rich.

Costantino Rocca

It's funny how circumstances sometimes transpire to lead us in unexpected directions. This tale recounts the chain of events that led me to the legendary Harvey Penick and the subsequent effects that encounter had on my life.

I was visiting an uncle I had not seen in many years, a golfer's kinship sort of thing. Uncle Norman introduced me to the game of golf, starting as his caddie. A miserable

experience, thanks to weather and other circumstances; I hated the game, and I didn't
take it up in earnest until the age of thirty-
five. Immediately, the golf bug bit me.
During this visit, I picked up a book lying on
the kitchen counter, Harvey Penick's Little
Green Book, *If You're a Golfer, You're My
Friend.* The book so impressed me, I read it
cover to cover that night and decided to
meet Mr. Penick. Now was as good a time as
any.

From South Florida, I drove the following
week to Austin, Texas. After checking into a
motel on a Sunday night, I looked up his
phone number and anxiously placed the
call. I knew that Penick was old and frail,
but I was shocked to learn his current con-
dition. Helen Penick informed me that her
dear husband was "released from the hospital that very day and he was not expected to
make it." It was even more surprising that
she said to call in the morning and if he felt
up to it, "Mr. Penick would be happy to see
you." I was given directions to the house
and instructed to call around 10 A.M.

My emotions surged. At first, I felt sorry
for myself. I had driven fifteen hundred

miles, and I expected that effort would get me the audience I came for. I began to feel guilty, knowing how selfish that was. Saying a prayer, for Mr. Penick and myself, I retired early.

Arising at the crack of dawn the next morning, I restlessly waited for 10 o'clock to arrive. Precisely at 10, I began dialing, and for what seemed an eternity, I heard busy signals. The worst crossed my mind. *Was he even sicker? Did he die?* Paranoid that I am, I even thought that the phone was intentionally left off the hook to discourage my calling. At 11, I drove to the house.

Following precise directions, I arrived at the Penick home, situated in a beautiful part of town. Worried about coming before calling, I sheepishly knocked on the door. When a nurse answered, I asked for Mrs. Penick. She was out shopping, but the nurse asked if I would like to visit with Mr. Penick. After traveling such a long distance I was aching to say yes, but I declined. "I think I'd better wait to see if it's okay with Mrs. Penick first." The next several hours were awe-inspiring and would change the course of my personal and professional life.

Outside, in this pristine setting, I became aware of changes, faint at first, in my sensory perceptions. The colors of the flowers were distinctive and bright. A gentle breeze blowing, the air was crisp and clear. Rich, pleasant aromas abounded. I heard several birds and could distinguish the differences in each of their songs. My body tingling all over, I was captivated by a heightened sense of awareness, actually feeling a part of nature. For a cold, calculating, bottom-line guy like me, this experience was a first.

I remember seeing a squirrel on the opposite side of the street. I closed my eyes, believing the squirrel would come closer, and to my delight he did. Closing my eyes again, I knew he would come right beside me. Well, nobody's perfect. This trancelike state lasted for what seemed an eternity, yet in reality was only thirty minutes or so. Mrs. Penick arrived and asked me to come in.

The bedroom resembled a hospital ward with tubes and machines everywhere. Mr. Penick was glad that I had come, eager to talk golf and share his wisdom. His love for the game was obvious, and talking about golf seemed to lift his spirits. A glow enveloped him as he shared with me a lifetime of teaching, people and stories. He asked about my personal life, my game, and how he might help me. What we discussed is almost irrelevant, for I knew that I was in the presence of greatness.

His son Tinsley stopped by the house, and our session continued. From his deathbed—he would pass away the following week—Mr. Penick was giving me a golf lesson. Incredibly perceptive, from our conversation, he could detect my flaws. After a few hours, I could see how tired he had become, so I excused myself to see if I should go. Though Mr. Penick wanted to continue, Tinsley felt it was time for rest. I thanked them all and left. How remarkable this family is. At a time when most people would only think of themselves and their troubles, they welcomed me into their home as if I was a lifelong friend. I made a conscious decision to live my life and play the game of golf according to a higher principle, Harvey Penick's way. Meeting him altered my life.

To make a long story short, that encounter led to my writing *The Secrets to the*

Game of Golf & Life, for which Tinsley agreed to write the foreword. I still get goose bumps every time I read it. Among other thoughts in his foreword, Tinsley wrote that his father and I became "kindred spirits and soul brothers" and that "Leonard has brought that special feeling to the pages of his new book." I am now firmly entrenched in the golf community, as a writer and consultant. Meeting Harvey Penick helped me to become a better golfer, but more importantly, a better person. I look at both golf and life from a different perspective, more aware and more appreciative.

Leonard Finkel

Snakes Alive!

Golf is temporary insanity practiced in a pasture.

DAVE KINDRED

Dave Harris, my roommate and golfing partner in college, was almost a scratch golfer. He would have been invited to play on the university team except for one frailty; he was an incorrigible practical joker. Sometimes it was the duck call he blew during somebody's backswing, but mostly it came from the collection of rubber snakes in his golf bag. One afternoon, a burly freshman from Spokane lined up a putt on the 6th hole, but backed off when, out of the corner of his eye, he spied a nasty-looking articulated python lying on the green. "Harris," he said, "you pull this stuff again and I'll part that blond crew cut with a 5-iron and reduce your fat frame to blubber!" So Dave laid off for a while, but one afternoon while playing as a twosome at Green Hill Country Club, he caused a big black snake with yellow stripes to appear suddenly at my feet just as I was about to tee off.

Then in the spring of 1947, Dave and I parted company. I took a job with the Montana State Highway Department, but he stuck around at the University of Washington to go for his masters; I ended up on a sizable construction job working out of Shelby in northern Montana. Shelby's major claim to fame was having been the scene of the infamous Dempsey/Gibbons prize fight in 1923; a gigantic billboard on the road into town told the passing world about it. Its other notable feature was that it was one of the few prairie towns up along the High-Line to sport a real municipal golf course.

The course was singularly spartan in its configuration. The locals had simply mowed down a few acres of buffalograss for fairways, set the mower as low as it would go to make greens, dragged in an old granary for a starter's shack, and voila!—instant golf course. But they had to dig the cups about two feet deep so the wind wouldn't blow the flagsticks over, and most short putts were conceded because nobody relished the idea of reaching up to the elbow into those dark recesses for a ball. Also, a lot of the mowing and some of the fertilizing was accomplished by allowing a local rancher to graze a few scrawny old cows on the place. I had tried playing the course twice but gave up in disgust both times, once after nicking the dickens out of a brand-new 8-iron on a rock and the other because the tumbleweeds, running before a Wild West wind, sailed across my line of sight every time I set up to swing. But there was no waiting, since the course was always completely deserted until the weekends, when one of the cattle owner's kids kicked the cows out to another pasture and then opened up the starter's shack and accepted two-dollar green fees from a few hardy souls.

Dave and I had kept in touch, and one evening he called saying he was working at Glacier Park for the summer and invited me up for a round of golf whenever I was free. "Davey," I said, "I'd love to, but we're working seven-day weeks right now. But, heck, we've got a perfectly good course right here in Shelby; I can take off a little early one day and we can play some twilight golf. After all, it doesn't get dark up here until about ten during July, and you're only a two-hour drive away."

"Great! How about this Wednesday? Thursday's my day off."

"Fine. See you then, ol' buddy."

First I reserved a room for Dave at the hotel, then made a small purchase in the novelty section of the drugstore and dropped in for a short chat with Tom, proprietor of Tommy's Bar and Grill. Then I located Jimmy, the kid who insisted on riding shotgun whenever I went out of town because he loved to watch heavy equipment move earth.

"Jimmy," I said, "do you think you could find a couple of snakes somewhere by Wednesday afternoon? Any kind, as long as they are good-sized and not rattlers."

"Sure. How about gopher snakes? There's a bunch of 'em living under our chicken house."

"Beautiful," I said, and handed him a piece of paper with instructions along with a dollar bill. "And there's another buck in it if you do a good job."

Dave showed up at the hotel right on time, and on the way to the golf course he said, "Bob, I know I used to give you strokes back in Seattle, but here you have all the local knowledge, so how about playing this round even-steven and just for a couple of beers?"

I said okay, and while Dave surveyed the course from the 1st tee with a certain air of misgiving, I said, "Davey, you're a city guy and this is a country course, so I think I owe you some pointers. First of all, I notice the cattle are grazing out here this evening, so I'd suggest you either take off or cover up that red shirt. Also, if your ball comes to rest on or within six inches of a cow it can be lifted without penalty. And I should point out that this is rattlesnake country, and they start coming out this time of day, so please watch your step; the nearest antivenom clinic is ninety miles away."

So, although it was still about eighty degrees in the shade, Dave pulled a blue sweater out of his bag. Then, despite glancing over his shoulder at the cows every five seconds and scanning the grass for snakes, he managed to hit to within a couple feet off the green in three on the par-4 1st hole. He sank a twenty-foot chip. "Bobby," he said as he pulled out the pin, "I think I've already begun to figure out your little course." But when he reached for the ball and his fingers encountered the cool coils of a big snake moving around looking for daylight, he flung his 6-iron away, tried to run but stumbled, fell on his behind and lay there gasping for breath. "Bob," he whispered, "I think there's some kind of snake in there!"

I looked in the hole, reached down, grabbed the animal by the neck, turned him loose to the prairie and, as he slithered away, said, "Heck, Davey, he's just an ol' gopher snake. Wouldn't hurt a soul. In fact, folks like to have 'em around because they eat mice and rats."

On the next hole, another par-4, Dave

regained composure, hit a lucky shot out of a clump of cactus and actually scored a birdie. Then on the 3rd, a 175-yard par-3, his tee shot landed in the only "sand trap" on the course, a natural alkali seep which had probably been there for a few thousand years, and Dave ended with a terrible lie. But he laid open a sand wedge, blasted out to within three feet of the pin, and was about to putt out when the handsome head of another gopher snake poked itself over the edge of the hole, stuck its tongue out at Dave, and then fell back. "Hey, Bob," he yelled, "there's another one of your pet snakes trapped in here!"

I trotted up to the hole, peered in and said, "Davey, this one happens to be a rattlesnake with six rattles on his tail, and I don't understand why he didn't buzz at you. But if you had come any closer, we might have been on our way to the clinic in Great Falls. So for the rest of the round, why don't we just concede any putts under four feet? And I hope that wasn't a new ball." Then while Dave shakily marked down the scores, I reminded myself to slip little Jimmy an extra buck. He had performed well.

After that, all the wheels came off Dave's game, and at the end of nine holes he flung away his sweater, gazed at his new white shoes covered with cow dung and said, "Well, Bobby, I've had it with your damned country golf course, and the beer is on me."

Later, sitting at the bar in Tommy's Bar and Grill, Dave lifted his first mug of cold suds, hesitated, looked again into the glass and then reeled back in disgust. There in the bottom rested a little rubber snake, coiled and ready to strike.

After a couple of deep breaths, he looked around the room at all the quiet, expectant faces, reached into the mug with two fingers and extracted the snake. Then he drained the beer and said loudly, "Tommy, would you put a head on this? But you don't need to be so fancy with the next one. I'll just have it plain without a snake." The regulars, primed ahead for this event, gave him an ovation. One anonymous patron must have been really impressed, because somebody picked up the dinner tab that night.

I said good-bye to Dave early while he was in deep conversation with Lucy, the waitress, because I had to get up at five in the morning. The next afternoon back at the hotel, Bill, the desk clerk/manager/owner, hailed me in the lobby and handed me a note from Dave:

"Dear ol' buddy—I got to know little Lucy pretty well last night, and she ratted on you. It was all nicely orchestrated, but did you really need to get half the town involved? Anyhow, you made your point. Looking forward to another round on a course as far away as possible from yours.

—Dave."

I tucked the note in my shirt pocket and started for the room and a shower, but Bill stopped me and said, "By the way, your friend must be into novelties or toys or something."

"Nope," I said. "He's a dumb engineer like myself."

"Well, it's strange. He didn't check out until just before noon, and when Hilda finally got in to make up his room, she came down all excited because he left a dozen rubber snakes in the wastebasket."

Bob Brust

Fear of the Father-Son Tournament

It is in the blood of genius to love play for its own sake, and whether one uses one's skill on thrones or women, swords or pens, gold or fame, the game's the thing.

GELETT BURGESS

No words strike greater fear in the occasional playing offspring of the inveterate golfer than these: father-son tournaments. For years, my father's mistaken assumption that I needed a valid handicap kept me off the hook. But when he learned otherwise, there was no escape. A date was set, a starting time inked.

Occasional playing is an overstatement,

though years ago (fourth and fifth grades) I did live on the 15th hole of an Oklahoma City course. Consequently, I learned a lot: how to duck, and that some of the worst shankers in the world reside just east of the Texas panhandle. I had my first taste of the game then. Dad would take me out after dusk, and we'd play the closing holes. If I shot my age on a hole, I was thrilled.

My game peaked a few years later when I tagged along on my neighbor's trips to South Carolina every summer. We played almost every day. There's no pressure to perform in front of someone else's dad. What do they care if you stink? It's not a reflection on their gene pool.

Outside of one glorious 94 in high school, my game has been in decline ever since. I play once or twice a year, three times if I'm lucky.

Dad, on the other hand, plays once or twice a week. He's a legit 12 or 13 handicap who's known for his long drives, despite a backswing that cannot be captured by time-lapse photography.

He assured me that we would get out on the course a few times before the tourney.

And sure enough, two days before the big day, I set foot on the tee box for the first time.

It wasn't pretty. My scorecard sported more snowmen than a Minneapolis suburb in January. The putting display was the worst you'll see this side of a drunk on a miniature course at two in the morning. And, yes, despite using a driver half the size of my head, I whiffed, which, in terms of athletic ineptness, is surpassed only by striking out in kickball.

Still, there was hope. I didn't bean any deer. I found more balls than I lost. And off the tee, I wasn't looking too bad.

Have you ever tried to cram for the dentist? You brush, floss and gargle your brains out for two days trying to make up for six months of neglect. Well, this was me hours before the tournament. Poring over golf magazines, I'm putting in the basement and perusing the tube for tips—or at least a rerun of *Dead Solid Perfect, Tin Cup* or even *Caddyshack.*

Given my antics, you'd think my father was exerting a lot of pressure on me. Not at all. Sure, doing well would enhance the experience, but he just wants to have fun.

Step onto that tee, though, and it's Little League all over again. You want to do well in front of Dad. Back when I was in high school we played tennis against two guys who together were about a century and a half old. They cleaned our clock as I sprayed balls everywhere but on the court. And tennis is my better sport.

D-day rolls around and the weather is beautiful. I discover that Dad has put me in for a 26 handicap, even though the last time I saw the 90s was in, well, the '80s. Add his legit 13 handicap, multiply by 40 percent, and we get sixteen shots. It won't be enough.

While at the pro shop, he tries to buy me a new pair of golf shoes. My game doesn't deserve it, but one of the man's great joys in life is buying athletic footwear for family, so I relent. Without the old fifteen pounds of foot gear, the only thing left to keep my head down is a self-imposed burden of expectation.

We arrive at the 1st tee, and my fear of being paired with Johnny Miller and son disappears. It's a mother and son, and they're getting twenty shots. Maybe this will be okay after all.

The format: Both partners hit tee shots

and then you alternate shots from the better of the two. After a spectator makes the requisite mulligan crack, I step up and pop up to short right. I half expect someone to invoke the infield fly rule, but no one does and the ball lands safely on the edge of the fairway. The mighty Casey has not whiffed!

We play my drive. Dad sticks it on the green; I almost drop the putt. Par! I crush the tee ball at the 2nd, and we make another par. We bogey the 3rd and then make a third par. Images of a net 54 and a club championship dance through my head. I am Tiger Woods!

Then reality rears its ugly head, and the train wreck begins: double bogey, bogey, triple, double, double. We briefly recover on the back nine and then fade. As the rain begins to fall, we struggle home with a 90, net 74. The mother-son combo takes us by two.

I have not led us to greatness. Nor have I let us down. I've simply been the mediocre golfer that I am, sharing a cart, a score and an all-too-rare afternoon with my old man. And that is plenty.

Besides, there's always next year. I might

take lessons, hit the driving range and trade my running magazine subscription for golf. Maybe hit the course every Sunday and get that handicap. Then again, perhaps I'll just dust off my clubs (and those new shoes) in time for next year's tournament.

Mike Pennella

The Y2K Crisis

In order to get as much fame as one's father, one has to be much more able than he.

DENIS DIDEROT

Some of you may be unaware of the crisis on our horizon. Let this be the moment you learn.

As the new millennium approaches, a threat looms—a threat so ominous and far-reaching, its reversal will require every ounce of ingenuity, every fiber of resolve and every corpuscle of human courage. Otherwise, panic—and ultimately devastation—surely will ensue.

I'm referring, of course, to the situation in my household—more specifically, to the nasty business with the younger of my two sons, Scott.

I remember back when Scott was eight years old, an age when every nonsclaffed shot was cause for joy, when to ride in an E-Z-GO was to live large and when the world's number-one golfer was Dad.

Oh, how things have changed. I forget whether it was Mark Twain or Will Rogers who said, "When I was fourteen, my father was a complete idiot. By the time I reached twenty-one, I was astounded at how much the old man had learned." Well, Scott is now fourteen.

And so is his handicap. In two years he's shaved twenty strokes. Although he can't hit the ball as far as I can—at least he couldn't last year—his swing is far smoother and produces better contact. His short game is sharper than that of any other 14-handicapper I know, and his putting nerves are, well, those of a fourteen-year-old. And he knows it.

So these days, when I hit a drive long and straight, I hear no "Wow!" from the sidelines, just an occasional snort. And when my three-footer rims the cup, he doesn't commiserate, he snickers.

Scott and I are no longer teammates, we're enemies. Indeed, for almost a year now, the little snit has been laboring under the gross misconception that, over a given eighteen holes, he can actually beat me. Beat me! Even up!

You can't imagine how annoying it is when, every time you tee it up with a person, he announces, "Today, you're going *down*." Well, let me tell you, that is just not going to happen. At least not any time soon. After all, despite creeping decrepitude, I can still scrape it around my home course in under 80 as often as not, while Scott's best is well, okay, 81—but let's face it, that day the fairways were hard as rocks, and he also drained everything he looked at.

Anyway, near the end of last summer I became so fed up with his insolence that I issued a solemn oath. "Scott," I said, "you will not beat me this year. You will not beat me next year. Indeed, you will not beat me this century or, for that matter, this millennium. I will hold you off until at least the first day of 2000."

Smart aleck that he is, he immediately

smirked, "The year 2000 is part of the twentieth century, Dad."

"Fine, you will not beat me in any year that starts with 1."

And so the battle has been joined. Filial piety is dead, intergenerational strife reigns, as father and son gird themselves for a season of grimly serious combat. An Oedipal thing is going on, too, as my dear wife has positioned herself firmly behind her son.

I don't care. There's no way that half-pint is going to dethrone me. He might get lucky for nine holes again, the way he did last fall, but hey, neither of us had ever seen that course, and he needed an ignorance-is-bliss 38 to do it. And I can assure you I will never again allow him to take a three-stroke lead with two holes to go. I was incredibly distracted by office stuff that day. Besides, he flat-ass choked on 17 and 18.

Believe me, it ain't gonna happen. Scott won't start playing regularly until school's out, while I plan to get in at least a dozen rounds before then, maybe even a quick lesson. I think I may need a little less loft on my driver, too. But I'll get that all fixed, rest assured.

Yep, as long as he doesn't hit his growth spurt before June, as long as he keeps sandwedging shots that should be bumped-and-run, and as long as no one tells him his irons need regripping, I like my chances.

In fact, nothing gives me more pleasure than the notion of battling that little bugger for the remainder of this century—and a long way into the next.

Come and get me, Son.

George Peper

[EDITORS' NOTE: *George Peper held out until late November of 1999 when he choked on the 18th hole with a double-bogey to lose to his son for the first time. But that was during a vacation trip to Japan, so he decided it didn't count! Then in the last week of December, his son threw a 74 at him to beat him soundly. At this writing their handicaps are both five, but George's is on the way up and his son's is coming down.*]

Thursday Is Men's Day

A state judge has put a Massachusetts country club under direct court supervision, saying compelling evidence at trial showed systematic sex discrimination that warranted judicial oversight in the public interest. The judge will personally oversee putting new policies into effect at Haverhill Golf and Country Club.

—News item, January 2000

Owing to a harsh winter and business overload in the spring, it had been close to four months since I'd been out to my country club, so you can imagine my surprise when I drove up and saw all the surreys with the fringe on top. They were lined up where the golf carts used to be.

I parked under an oak and immediately went over to speak to the cart boy, who was now a girl. "Do you work here, miss?" I asked.

"I'm the cart person, yes," she said, eating yogurt out of a cup and leaning on a carousel horse that was attached to a surrey. "I'm Ellen."

"You're new, Ellen."

"Yeah. I was hired after James got karate chopped."

"James got what?"

"He called Francesca 'honey,' or 'babe' or something like that, so she gave him a karate chop in the neck and fired him."

"Who's Francesca?"

"You don't know Francesca? She's the head pro."

"She is? What happened to Dutch?"

"Dutch who?"

"Dutch Miller. He's been the pro here for fifteen years."

"There's a Dutch who works in the kitchen."

"Dutch is the chef now?"

"I'm not sure you'd call a dishwasher a chef."

As calmly as possible, I said, "Tell me, Ellen. By what set of, shall I say, bizarre circumstances did somebody named Francesca get to be our head pro?"

"I don't know. You'd have to ask Juliette."

"Juliette . . . ?"

"Boy, you haven't been around here in a while, have you? Juliette's the director of golf."

I stormed into the golf shop and went over to a young woman behind the counter. "Are you Francesca?"

"I'm Samantha. Francesca's playing in a tournament this week."

"Where's Juliette?"

"She's playing in the same tournament."

I looked around. The shop was mostly stocked with women's clubs and women's apparel.

Heavy on the sarcasm, I said, "Do you have any fuchsia Titleists?"

"No, but we have egg yolk and lime," she said seriously.

I decided I needed a drink, a double Junior, and went around to the men's grill. Only the large sign above the door said it was now called Emily's Cafe.

"Hi, I'm a member," I said to the woman who greeted me. "I see the room has a new name, but I assume I can still get a cocktail."

"Only on Thursdays, I'm afraid," the woman said.

I countered, "You're telling me I can only come in here on Thursdays?"

"Thursday is men's day on the golf course. Naturally, you can drink and dine in here on Thursdays. You're not familiar with the new club rules? They've been in the monthly club bulletins."

"I guess I should have been reading them."

"Yes, I dare say you should have."

"Are you Emily?"

"No, I'm Dorothy. Emily's playing in a tournament this week."

"What if I hit your palm with a little whip-out, Dorothy? Do you suppose that would help me get a drink?"

"Tipping is not allowed, sir."

"What about begging? Is that permissible?"

"Sir, I will be happy to send a drink around to you in the men's locker room. It's where the women's used to be, of course."

"Of course."

I had my drink in what was now the small and cramped men's locker room, where an attendant told me he could bring me a zucchini and beet sandwich if I was hungry. I declined limply.

When I went outside to leave I found two female security guards standing by my car. One of them said, "You parked in Francesca's spot."

"Sorry," I said. "I didn't know."

"You'll know next time," she said.

I drove home on four punctured tires and desperately started looking in storage closets for my old croquet set.

Dan Jenkins

Humor at Its Best

I had a wonderful experience on the golf course today. I had a hole in nothing. Missed the ball and sank the divot.

DON ADAMS

Hartman was a big man. Physically, he was a solid 280 pounds and stood around six-foot-two. He had a presence about him that demanded attention when he entered a room, and he had a twinkle in his eye. Oh, that twinkle! Hartman was the kind of man who could talk a half dozen men into walking outside in the snow in their bare feet, and still be in position to close the door and lock it, before he actually had to go out himself.

Hartman was the person who introduced me to golf. He loved the game. On one occasion, when we were younger, a group of us rented a farmhouse for the summer. It was a place where we could go at the end of the week and just do whatever comes to mind. Hartman suggested one evening that we go to the local golf course the following day and play a round. Eight of us agreed immediately and went off to bed at a reasonable hour, which at the time was not the norm, so we could get an early start.

The next morning we arrived at the golf course early enough to be the first two groups off. Being a small "farmers field" type of golf course we fit right in. The skill level of all the participants varied from just above beginner to really struggling for a bogey round. Hartman was one of the more accomplished players out that day, but it was obvious that he was struggling along with the rest of us.

Finally, after the increasing frustration seemed to win out, Hartman snapped! He stood up on the tee of the par-3, 157-yard 8th hole and pulled his driver from his bag. With a great deal of drama, for which

Hartman was known, he pulled back on that club and pasted that poor ball with every ounce of his 280 pounds. The ball took off as if it knew it was no longer wanted and headed straight for the trees and the river just to the left of the hole. By this time the other group had already joined us on the tee and the seven of us were howling with laughter. No one really tracked the ball except Hartman, who cringed as we all heard the ball hit a tree to the left of the green. What none of us were ready for was the look on his face as he excitedly asked us, "Did you see that?"

"See what?" was the common reply.

"My ball. It came off that tree, bounced off that rock in front of the green and rolled towards the pin. I think I'm close!"

"Yeah, right. That ball was so far gone you'll never find it," I said with a note of finality.

Fully convinced that there was no way in the world Hartman's ball was even on the golf course any more, let alone anywhere near the hole, we watched as Hartman teed up what we considered to be his serious ball. He hit it fat with his 8-iron, and we all started to walk toward the green disregarding everything he had to say about it being a provisional ball.

As we approached the green we were giving Hartman a pretty hard time. It was becoming more and more obvious his ball wasn't on the green. Hartman couldn't believe it.

"I know I saw it head in this direction," he said with absolute conviction.

"Maybe it's in the hole!" suggested Pete in a sarcastic tone.

Pete walked up to the hole, looked down and yelled back to Hartman.

"What are you hitting?"

"Top Flite number 4" was Hartman's reply.

You could have knocked Pete over with a feather as he leaned over and picked the ball out of the hole.

"It's in the hole," was all he was able to stammer.

Hartman was the last one of us to arrive at the hole to authenticate the ball.

"That's it. I don't believe it! A hole-in-one!" he exclaimed excitedly.

The rest of us just stood there with our

mouths open and looks of utter disbelief on our faces. It wasn't possible, yet seven of us witnessed it. The most incredible shot in history.

We finished our round in a state of excited numbness, anxiously waiting to tell someone, anyone, what we had witnessed.

Back at the clubhouse we were indulging in a few beers and regaling the story among ourselves and anyone else who would listen. That's when someone suggested we call the local newspaper and maybe get our pictures taken and enjoy our fifteen minutes of fame. While we were planning all the TV appearances and endorsement contracts, Hartman sat at the end of the table with that twinkle in his eye. Oh, that twinkle! It was the unmistakable tone of his laugh at that point that removed all doubt. We had been duped!

Being the first group off that morning put us in the unique position of being the first to each hole. Hartman took advantage of that fact when playing the 6th hole, which paralleled the 8th.

Having hit his ball in the narrow stretch of woods between the two holes, no one thought anything of his activities while he was looking for his ball. While wandering around in this no-man's-land he meandered over to the 8th green, casually dropped his ball in the hole and then wandered back to the 6th fairway as if he had just played his ball out of the rough. The rest of that hole and the next one leading up to the 8th was a display of acting on a Shakespearean level, to bring his apparent frustration level to a peak on the 8th tee.

The number of people with the imagination and savvy to pull off a prank of this magnitude and make all his victims feel good about being had are few and far between. This was the case with most of his pranks, the ones who laughed hardest were the ones at the center of the prank. We lost Hartman to cancer at the young age of forty-three, but he left behind a legacy of good-natured humor, a zest for life and a true appreciation of the good friends he had.

I miss the big man.

John Spielbergs

The Life and Times
of a Golf Ball

I have talked to golf balls all my golfing life. I accept that a golf ball is inanimate; I understand that a golf ball does not have ears or a brain or even a nervous system. But it is, nonetheless, pleasing to see a golf ball pop right out of a bunker at the exact moment you've yelled, "Skip, golf ball, skip!" So, yes, I talk to golf balls; I admit to that. If I had to guess, I'd say we talkers are in the majority.

MICHAEL BAMBERGER

There is nothing surprising about it—ending up in this trash can behind the golf shop. I suppose it was inevitable from the day they put me in a package back at the factory. Still it's deeply disappointing: Nobody or nothing in the world likes to admit that the end is near. Not even a golf ball.

A golf ball? That's right. So no golf ball has spoken out until now. Well, I'm going to tell my story. It needs telling—too many of us have been sliced, hooked, topped, scuffed and thrown to oblivion without a backward glance from the people we have served so loyally.

My life hasn't been typical, because for one splendid day I had the kind of life few golf balls enjoy—a chance to perform on the professional tour. But, other than that I've been the same as my brothers. Now, battered, bruised and severely cut I have been tossed out—worthless.

My last few weeks were spent on the practice range. A horrid kind of existence. You're poured into a bucket, then dumped onto the ground and clubbed down-range by golfers with talents ranging from lots of it to none at all.

But I was surviving all right until this morning. A lady beginner talked briefly with the pro before picking up the bucket of balls where I was resting. "I never have played golf before, but my husband insists that I give it a try," the lady explained to the pro. I winced.

She was dangerous, the kind who could deliver a fatal blow with one disjointed swing. My only hope was that she would hit the ground behind me so I could dribble along the grass and avoid serious damage. There wasn't a prayer that she would hit me square.

I watched painfully as she chopped away, missing some balls two or three times.

Finally my turn came, and she flailed at me with a 7-iron. It might as well have been an axe. The clubhead hit into my topside, and I would have screamed in agony if the golf ball code of ethics had permitted.

Instead, I needed all my strength and determination to hold my tightly wound innards in place as I skittered along the ground. The pain was almost unbearable, but I turned numb as I rolled to a stop less than thirty yards from the tee.

I took a hurried inventory and learned the worst—I had a mortal wound, a deep and ugly gash that laid bare my wrappings and assured the end of even my driving range days.

Less than an hour later I was picked up by the range boy. He took one look at me and, without hesitation, dumped me in a sack with other discards. A little later he tossed me into this trash can.

But that's only the end of the story, the saddest chapter. I would like to tell the whole thing, including the part about my close relationship with Sandy Douglas, the famous touring pro.

By some kind of a lucky break, I was given to Sandy by the sporting goods salesman. Sandy uses only balls with the number 3 on them, and that's my number. So into his bag I went just two days before the $200,000 Dorado Classic.

Several new balls were in the bag, but not so many that I couldn't be sure to see action. Sandy, like most of the pros, uses a ball for only six holes or so before switching it to his practice bag. I was delighted. I would compete in a major tournament, and then I would serve out my life with Sandy Douglas, traveling in a shag bag from city to city on the Tour.

Well, things started out just as I expected. Actually, they started even better, because Sandy picked me out as one of the first three balls he would use in the Classic. I got in on the preliminary action, too—he used me for his tuneup on the putting green.

Sandy Douglas is all the things everybody says about him. He's colorful, humorous, and he has the kind of charm that draws big galleries: there must have been five thousand people crammed around the 1st tee to watch him. Sandy placed me carefully on a tee and then took his address position. I was tingling all over.

"Okay, little ball, let's just send you out there nice and easy," Sandy said quietly, and then he swung smoothly. The driver came into me perfectly, and suddenly the green color below me was a blur. I reached my peak height and started down. I could feel myself being drawn to the middle of the fairway, and finally, I bumped down and rolled to a stop.

The spectators were applauding, and I could see that we were in perfect position, about 275 yards out and with a clear shot to the green. Sandy and his caddie strolled up, held a brief conference on distance and club selection, and then I was on my way again, this time with a 9-iron. Again the swing was good and I climbed into a high arc before dropping toward the flagstick. Sandy had been a little firm with me, but I managed to dig into the green and curl back to within eight feet of the hole.

A small coin was placed behind me and the caddie gave me a bath before Sandy placed me back on the green and prepared to putt. He wanted a birdie for a fast start, and I wanted to help him get it.

"It looks as if it will break about an inch to the left," Sandy said to the caddie.

"A little more than that, about an inch and a half," the caddie replied.

Sandy didn't say any more. He carefully lined me up and a hush settled all around. Finally, he tapped me, and I rolled gingerly towards the cup. Two feet away I began to break to the left, and I was dead on line. *Plunk!* In I went, and a huge roar arose from the spectators. Sandy picked me out of the cup and held me up to acknowledge the cheers. It was the supreme moment for me.

The 2nd hole was another par-4, and

Sandy gave me another good ride off the tee, but with a bit more hook than he wanted. I ended up in the rough, but I managed to crawl into a good lie and there was no problem. A solid 8-iron put me six feet from the hole on a flat portion of the green. It was a straight-in putt and Sandy sank me for another birdie.

Two holes and 2 under par! I could hardly believe it! It was an exquisite experience; I had to be the luckiest ball in the world—or so I thought.

Little did I know that heartbreak was just ahead. What hurts most is that it really wasn't the fault of either of us.

The 3rd hole is a par-3 of 180 yards with a pond right in front of the green.

"Give me the 6-iron," Sandy said.

"I think a 7-iron is enough," the caddie replied.

Then Sandy and the caddie huddled and I couldn't hear what they said, but when Sandy addressed me I could see he was using the 7-iron. The caddie had convinced him.

The next few seconds turned into sheer horror. Sandy hit me well, but from the moment I left the tee I could see that flying over that pond would be touch and go. If only he had stuck with that 6-iron.

I sailed through the air and started my descent. Everywhere I looked was water! Suddenly I was sick; I wasn't going to make it over the pond. With a knifing dive, I splashed into slimy weeds about three feet from the edge of the pond. I can't describe the agony I felt as I settled into the mud two feet under water.

A few minutes later I saw the head of a wedge poking about near me. Sandy was trying to find me, and I wanted desperately to reach out for that wedge, but of course I couldn't. Moments later, the wedge disappeared. I had been given up for lost.

Such was the end of the exciting part of my life. It was so brief, but so memorable.

What followed was almost predictable. About a week later a young boy was wading in the pond looking for balls. He found me along with a lot of others, sold some of the balls at the golf shop, but kept me. I still looked as good as new.

For the next month I served the boy's father, about a 12-handicapper who beat me up a bit but didn't give me any of those dreaded cuts. Finally he lost me in long grass behind a green. The next time I was found was by a greenskeeper who narrowly missed running over me with his mower. He turned me over to the golf shop, and that started my tour of duty on the driving range.

That's about all there is to tell. I lived dangerously but made it by okay until the other day.

Now I'm buried deep in this trash can, and I can hear the garbage truck coming. I recognize the sound because I've heard it many times in the last few weeks.

It's just a matter of minutes now until they haul me away to the dump. I wonder how Sandy Douglas finished in the Dorado Classic. I wonder how my life might have gone if it hadn't been for that pond. I wonder if that lady beginner will ever learn to hit a ball.

Bob Robinson

Who Is Jack Canfield?

Jack Canfield is one of America's leading experts in the development of human potential and personal effectiveness. He is both a dynamic, entertaining speaker and a highly sought-after trainer. Jack has a wonderful ability to inform and inspire audiences toward increased levels of self-esteem and peak performance.

In addition to the *Chicken Soup for the Soul* series, Jack has coauthored numerous books, including his most recent release, *The Success Principles, How to Get From Where You Are to Where You Want to Be* with Janet Switzer, *The Aladdin Factor* with Mark Victor Hansen, *100 Ways to Build Self-Concept in the Classroom* with Harold C. Wells, *Heart at Work* with Jacqueline Miller and *The Power of Focus* with Les Hewitt and Mark Victor Hansen.

Jack is regularly seen on television shows such as Good Morning America, 20/20 and NBC Nightly News.

For further information about Jack's books, tapes and training programs, or to schedule him for a presentation, please contact:

Self-Esteem Seminars
P.O. Box 30880
Santa Barbara, CA 93130
Phone: 805-563-2935
Fax: 805-563-2945
www.chickensoup.com

Who Is Mark Victor Hansen?

In the area of human potential, no one is better known and more respected than Mark Victor Hansen. For more than thirty years, Mark has focused solely on helping people from all walks of life reshape their personal vision of what's possible.

He is a sought-after keynote speaker, bestselling author and marketing maven. Mark is a prolific writer with many bestselling books such as *The One Minute Millionaire, The Power of Focus, The Aladdin Factor* and *Dare to Win*, in addition to the *Chicken Soup for the Soul* series.

Mark has appeared on Oprah, CNN and The Today Show, and has been featured in *Time, U.S. News & World Report, USA Today, New York Times* and *Entrepreneur* and countless radio and newspaper interviews.

As a passionate philanthropist and humanitarian, he has been the recipient of numerous awards that honor his entrepreneurial spirit, philanthropic heart and business acumen.

For further information on Mark's products and services, please contact:

Mark Victor Hansen & Associates, Inc.
P.O. Box 7665
Newport Beach, CA 92658
Phone: 949-764-2640
Fax: 949-722-6912
FREE resources online at:
www.markvictorhansen.com

Who Is Jeff Aubery?

Introduced to the golf industry at an early age, Jeff was mentored personally and professionally by Nat C. Rosasco, owner of Northwestern Golf Co. Now an entrepreneur in his own right, Jeff founded and is the president of Golf Sales West, Inc./Tornado Golf, the world's largest original equipment golf bag manufacturer.

Jeff is most proud of his tireless work to help bring millions of people to the game of golf by developing programs and products that are accessible and affordable for everyone.

Jeff is an active sponsor of junior golf programs and charity golf tournaments all over the world. Jeff makes time for a round of golf whenever possible and has enjoyed playing with some of the greatest names in the sport at many of the world's most famous courses.

Jeff is coauthor of #1 *New York Times* bestsellers *Chicken Soup for the Golfer's Soul, Chicken Soup for the Father's Soul* and *Chicken Soup for the Golfer's Soul: The Second Round.* He is a veteran of hundreds of radio and television interviews.

He can be reached at:

Golf Sales West, Inc./Tornado Golf
2100 Eastman Ave., Suite A
Oxnard, CA 93030
phone: 800-GOLF-BAG
E-mail: *SoupStory@aol.com*

Who Are Mark & Chrissy Donnelly?

Avid golfers Mark and Chrissy Donnelly are the coauthors of the #1 *New York Times* bestsellers *Chicken Soup for the Couple's Soul, Chicken Soup for the Golfer's Soul, Chicken Soup for the Sports Fan's Soul, Chicken Soup for the Father's Soul* and *Chicken Soup for the Baseball Fan's Soul*. As cofounders of the Donnelly Marketing Group, they develop and implement innovative marketing and promotional strategies that help elevate and expand the *Chicken Soup for the Soul* message to millions of people around the world.

Mark was introduced to golf at the age of three. He remembers following his father to the golf course and finding a four-leaf clover that he believes enabled his father to win a prominent local amateur tournament. As a result of this and other golfing experiences with his father, Mark developed an appreciation for the game, along with a respectable golf game. Chrissy, COO of the Donnelly Marketing Group, also grew up in Portland, Oregon, and graduated from Portland State University. As a CPA, she embarked on a six-year career with Price Waterhouse. Contact:

    Donnelly Marketing Group, LLC
    2425 E. Camelback Road, Suite 515
    Phoenix, AZ 85016
    phone: 602-508-8956 fax: 602-508-8912
    E-mail: *chickensoup@cox.net*

Contributors

If you would like to contact any of the contributors for information about their writing or would like to invite them to speak in your community, look for their contact information, included in their biography.

Bob Brust, a native of Montana, worked as an engineer for Chevron U.S.A. for thirty-two years. After retiring, he pursued two of his greatest passions, writing and golf. His works have appeared in *Golf Journal, Chicken Soup for the Golfer's Soul,* several magazines and periodicals. He has also authored two books, *Idaho in June* and *I Thought I Heard a Rooster Crow.* The latter is about his life and his family on a ranch in Montana and is in the process of being published. Bob passed away in June 1999. Further information concerning his writing is available from Harriett Brust, *hebrust@iowatelecom.net.*

Jolee Edmondson writes about golf and many other subjects for national magazines. She is the only woman ever to have won a first-place award from the Golf Writers Association of America. A resident of Savannah, Georgia, she can be reached at *wordworx1@aol.com.*

Leonard Finkel, together with artist Gary Max Collins, produced *The Secrets to the Game of Golf & Life,* which contains fifty original oil painting by Collins. He is a freelance writer and editor of *Golf Journeys Magazine.* Leonard has had articles published in more than twenty magazines including *Golf Illustrated, Affluent Golfer* and almost a dozen cover stories for *Golf Today Magazine.* Leonard can be reached at *glfgd@aol.com* or visit the Web site at *www.golfandlife.com.*

Deisy Flood is originally from Cuba. She is married and has a son. She has contributed to *Golf Journal.* She resides in Lakeland, Florida, with her three dogs and owns a business. She loves golf, reading and writing. She is sorry her father didn't live to see her work, although not exactly professional, published. She can be reached at: *deisy_f@hotmail.com.*

Dan Jenkins, *Golf Digest* writer-at-large, is the author of seventeen novels and works of nonfiction, including two classic golf books, *The Dogged Victims of Inexorable Fate* and *Dead Solid Perfect.* He lives in his hometown of Fort Worth, Texas.

Mike Pennella is a runner, freelance writer and very occasional golfer residing in Maplewood, New Jersey. This story first appeared in *Golf Journal,* a magazine of the United States Golf Association. Proceeds from the reprinting of this story will be donated to the USGA Foundation.

George Peper is the editor-in-chief of *Golf* magazine. He is the author of a dozen books on golf, and his script for the PBS documentary *The Story of Golf* was nominated for an Emmy. His story was the impetus for his current book *Playing Partners,* about golf with his son, which will be published by Warner Books for Father's Day in 2003.

Bob Robinson a 1956 graduate of the University of Oregon, retired in 1999 after thirty-seven-and-a-half years as a sportswriter at *The Oregonian* in Portland, Oregon. He continues to do freelance writing, mostly on golf. He was named Oregon's Sportswriter of the Year in 1977 after covering the Portland Trail Blazers in their NBA championship season.

Bruce Selcraig, an Austin-based journalist, is a former U.S. Senate investigator and *Sports Illustrated* staff writer whose work has appeared in the *New York Times Magazine, Harper's* and *Sierra,* among others. He writes on topics as varied as corporate crime and baseball gloves, worships Irish golf and New Mexican food, and can be reached at *selcraig@swbell.net.*

John Spielbergs was born and raised in Toronto, Ontario. He currently is a custom homebuilder in Muskoka, a tourist area north of Toronto. He lives with his wife and two daughters and, in addition to golf, likes to play hockey. His story was written as a way of coming to terms with the loss of a life-long friend.

Supporting Others

A portion of the profits that are generated from sales of the original edition of the bestseller, *Chicken Soup for the Golfer's Soul, The 2nd Round*, published in 2002, will go to the Payne Stewart Family Foundation. Established in 1988, the purpose of the foundation is to primarily assist with programs that allow children and youth to have new opportunities to experience the joy of the Christian life.

The Payne Stewart Family Foundation
c/o Ronald Blue & Company
450 South Orange Avenue
Suite #250
Orlando, FL 32801

More Chicken Soup?

We enjoy hearing your reactions to the stories in *Chicken Soup for the Soul* books. Please let us know what your favorite stories were and how they affected you.

Many of the stories and poems you enjoy in *Chicken Soup for the Soul* books are submitted by readers like you who had read earlier *Chicken Soup for the Soul* selections.

We invite you to contribute a story to one of these future volumes.

Stories may be up to 1,200 words and must uplift or inspire. To obtain a copy of our submission guidelines and a listing of upcoming *Chicken Soup* books, please write, fax or check our Web sites.

Chicken Soup for the Soul
P.O. Box 30880
Santa Barbara, CA 93130
fax: 805-563-2945
Web site: *www.chickensoup.com*

Get inside the game

Code #267X • $9.95

Available wherever books are sold.
For a complete listing or to order direct:
Telephone (800) 441-5569 • Online www.hcibooks.com
Prices do not include shipping and handling. Your response code is CCS.

Real men read chicken

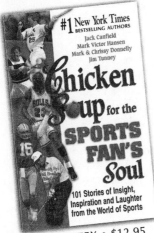

Code #875X • $12.95

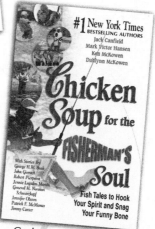

Code #1452 • $12.95

Available wherever books are sold.
For a complete listing or to order direct:
Telephone (800) 441-5569 • Online www.hcibooks.com
Prices do not include shipping and handling. Your response code is CCS.

Also Available

Chicken Soup African American Soul
Chicken Soup Body and Soul
Chicken Soup Bride's Soul
Chicken Soup Caregiver's Soul
Chicken Soup Cat and Dog Lover's Soul
Chicken Soup Christian Family Soul
Chicken Soup Christian Soul
Chicken Soup College Soul
Chicken Soup Country Soul
Chicken Soup Couple's Soul
Chicken Soup Expectant Mother's Soul
Chicken Soup Father's Soul
Chicken Soup Fisherman's Soul
Chicken Soup Girlfriend's Soul
Chicken Soup Golden Soul
Chicken Soup Golfer's Soul, Vol. I, II
Chicken Soup Horse Lover's Soul
Chicken Soup Inspire a Woman's Soul
Chicken Soup Kid's Soul
Chicken Soup Mother's Soul, Vol. I, II
Chicken Soup Nature Lover's Soul
Chicken Soup Parent's Soul
Chicken Soup Pet Lover's Soul
Chicken Soup Preteen Soul, Vol. I, II
Chicken Soup Single's Soul
Chicken Soup Soul, Vol. I-VI
Chicken Soup at Work
Chicken Soup Sports Fan's Soul
Chicken Soup Teenage Soul, Vol. I-IV
Chicken Soup Woman's Soul, Vol. I, II

Available wherever books are sold.
For a complete listing or to order direct:
Telephone (800) 441-5569 • Online www.hcibooks.com
Prices do not include shipping and handling. Your response code is CCS.